MINDFULNESS WITH

FAMILY

PRISCILLA AN

childsworld.com

The
Child's
World®
childsworld.com

Published by The Child's World®
800-599-READ · www.childsworld.com

Copyright © 2024 by The Child's World®
All rights reserved. No part of this book may be
reproduced or utilized in any form or by any means
without written permission from the publisher.

Photography Credits
Photographs ©: iStockphoto, cover, 1, 14–15, 16, 19, 20;
Shutterstock Images, 3, 5; Olena Yakobchuk/Shutterstock
Images, 6–7, 9, 10, 12–13; Dragon Images/Shutterstock
Images, 22

ISBN Information
9781503869615 (Reinforced Library Binding)
9781503880948 (Portable Document Format)
9781503882256 (Online Multi-user eBook)
9781503883567 (Electronic Publication)
9781645498698 (Paperback)

LCCN 2022951265

Printed in the United States of America

BRINGING THE WORLD
19 68
TO YOUNG READERS

Priscilla An is a children's book
editor and author. She lives in
Minnesota with her rabbit and
likes to practice mindfulness
through yoga.

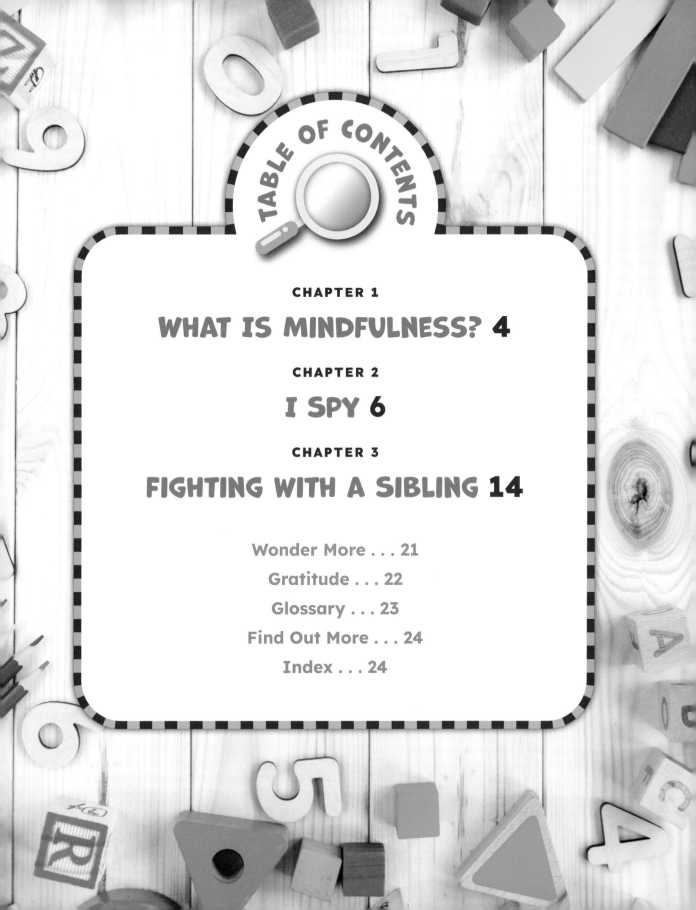

TABLE OF CONTENTS

WHAT IS MINDFULNESS?

Family relationships can be hard. Sometimes families fight. Mindfulness is when people pay attention to their thoughts, feelings, and surroundings. Being mindful can help people **focus** on the present moment. They are able to slow down. Slowing down helps people think about others. When people are mindful, they are able to be more **compassionate**. Compassion can be helpful when family members fight.

Families can practice mindfulness together during meals.

I SPY

Aiden's family is going on a trip. They are flying to visit Aiden's grandparents. Aiden is excited. He has never been on a plane before! When they arrive at the airport, Aiden's family goes through the **security checkpoint**. Aiden gets to stand in a big X-ray machine! Once they are through, Aiden's mom checks a big screen on the wall.

"Bad news, everyone," she says. "Our flight has been **delayed** for three hours. We will be here longer than we thought."

Vacations are a good time to bond with family members.

Aiden and his family settle into some empty chairs. One by one, Aiden reads all the books he brought along. He shifts positions in his chair. His body hurts from sitting too long. "When are we getting on the plane?" Aiden asks.

"We only have one hour left," his dad says.

"*Only*?" Aiden groans. One hour seems like a long time. "I am *so* bored." He puts his head on his suitcase. He wishes time would move faster.

STRETCHING

Sitting too long can make people's bodies hurt. Stretching can help. People can simply stand and reach their arms up high. Then they can try touching their feet.

Waiting can be hard.

Watching planes take flight can be exciting.

"Do you want to play a game together?" Aiden's dad asks. "When I was your age, my family played something called 'I Spy' during long trips."

Aiden sits up in his seat. A game sounds fun. "How do you play?"

"There is one spy in each round," Aiden's dad explains. "The spy needs to look around and pick an object. Then the spy says 'I spy. . .' and tells everyone a hint. The hint could be the color of the object or the first letter of the word. After that, everyone else can ask questions. They try to guess what the object is."

"Can I go first?" Aiden asks.

"Of course!" his dad says.

Aiden jumps to his feet. He wants to choose an object that is hard to guess. He sees his orange suitcase and pile of books. Too easy. Aiden looks carefully around him. A little girl is sleeping on her mom's lap. Lots of adults are drinking coffee. Aiden looks out the big windows. Airline workers in bright-yellow vests are loading people's **luggage** onto planes. He sees a plane take off into the blue sky.

With lots to do and see, airports can be fun!

Suddenly, Aiden sees a pilot walking up the stairs of an airplane. She is wearing a dark-blue suit with gold stripes on her sleeves. In her hand is a pilot's hat. "I've got it!" Aiden says excitedly. "I spy something that is dark-blue and gold."

As he plays the game with his parents, Aiden feels like time is going by faster. Playing the game helped him be more mindful of the things around him. That made him enjoy spending time with his parents. He did not focus so much on the long wait. Maybe he could play the game on the plane, too! There would be even more exciting things to see.

FIGHTING WITH A SIBLING

Camila just came home from school. She is excited to talk to her best friend, Emily. Emily moved away a month ago. Now, she and Emily video call almost every day.

After Camila drops her backpack in her room, she runs to the kitchen. She expects to see the tablet on the counter, but it is not there. She looks in the living room. Her brother Theo is using the tablet.

It is good to take breaks when playing on a phone or tablet.

Brothers and sisters do not always get along.

"Theo," Camila says, "I need the tablet!" Theo does not respond. He is playing a game. Camila knows she does not have to call Emily right away. But she still runs to the couch and grabs the tablet in Theo's hands. "I said I need to use the tablet!"

"Stop it!" Theo shouts. "It's *my* turn. I just started playing."

"But you're not doing anything important. You can use it later," Camila says. She tries to yank the tablet away. But Theo holds on tightly. He starts to cry.

"Camila." Their mom comes over. "Let Theo finish one game. Think about how he feels right now. Try to show some compassion."

Camila is angry that her mom is taking Theo's side. She wants to scream! But instead of reacting to her anger, Camila tries to think about Theo's **perspective**.

Camila closes her eyes. Her heart is beating fast. She takes a few slow breaths. As she breathes in, Camila feels her belly rise. She thinks about how Theo did not go to school today. He has been sick all week. This might be the first time he felt well enough to play. Camila breathes out.

By focusing on her breath, Camila's anger slowly fades away. She can think clearly. Camila decides to call Emily after Theo plays his game.

She gives the tablet back to Theo. "You can play. I'll wait for you." Theo hugs his sister and thanks her.

After Theo finishes, he gives the tablet to Camila. "Can I say hi to Emily, too?" he asks.

SELF-COMPASSION

It is important to show compassion to others. But being compassionate to oneself is just as important. People can practice self-compassion by treating themselves like a good friend. They can also learn to accept their emotions, even if those emotions are negative.

Taking turns helps people have fun.

Sharing is an act of kindness.

"Of course," Camila says. "I'm sorry that I shouted at you. I was too busy thinking about how I felt. You must have been so bored this week! I'm glad you feel better."

Theo smiles at Camila. "Thank you!" Camila smiles back at him. She is glad that she was more mindful of Theo's feelings. In her anger, she only thought about herself. Practicing mindfulness helped her think calmly. She was able feel compassion for her brother.

WONDER MORE

Wondering about New Information

How much did you know about the importance of mindfulness before reading this book? What new information did you learn? Write down two new facts that this book taught you. Was the new information surprising? Why or why not?

Wondering How It Matters

What is one way being mindful with family relates to your life? How do you think being mindful with family relates to other kids' lives?

Wondering Why

Showing compassion to others and to yourself is important. Why do you think it is important to do both? How might knowing this affect your life?

Ways to Keep Wondering

Learning about mindfulness with family can be a complex topic. After reading this book, what questions do you have about it? What can you do to learn more about mindfulness?

GRATITUDE

Gratitude means showing thankfulness. Try this simple gratitude activity with your family.

1 Have everyone say one thing that they are thankful for in their day. It can be as simple as, "I am thankful for the sun."

2 Next, have everyone say which family member they are thankful for and why.

GLOSSARY

compassionate (kum-PAH-shuh-nit) Being compassionate means showing kindness to another person, especially when the other person is having a hard time. Thinking of Theo's feelings helped Camila be compassionate.

delayed (deh-LAYD) To be delayed is to be slow or running late. Aiden's plane was delayed by three hours.

focus (FOH-kuss) To focus is to pay special attention to something. When Aiden played a game with his family, he did not focus on the long wait.

luggage (LUGG-ij) Luggage is the suitcases or other bags people often use for traveling. Workers store people's luggage in the bottom of an airplane.

perspective (per-SPEK-tiv) A perspective is a person's point of view. Considering Theo's perspective helped Camila feel sorry for her brother.

security checkpoint (seh-KYUR-ih-tee CHEK-poynt) Workers at a security checkpoint scan people and check bags to make sure no one is carrying anything dangerous. When people fly at airports, they have to pass through a security checkpoint.

stretching (STREH-ching) Stretching is extending parts of the body. Stretching can help make sore muscles feel better.

FIND OUT MORE

In the Library

An, Priscilla. *Mindfulness with Friends.*
Parker, CO: The Child's World, 2024.

DiOrio, Rana. *What Does It Mean to Be Present?*
Naperville, IL: Little Pickle Press, 2017.

Miller, Marie-Therese. *Families Like Mine.*
Minneapolis, MN: Lerner, 2021.

On the Web

Visit our website for links about mindfulness with family:
childsworld.com/links

Note to Parents, Caregivers, Teachers, and Librarians: We routinely verify our Web links to make sure they are safe and active sites. So encourage your readers to check them out!

INDEX